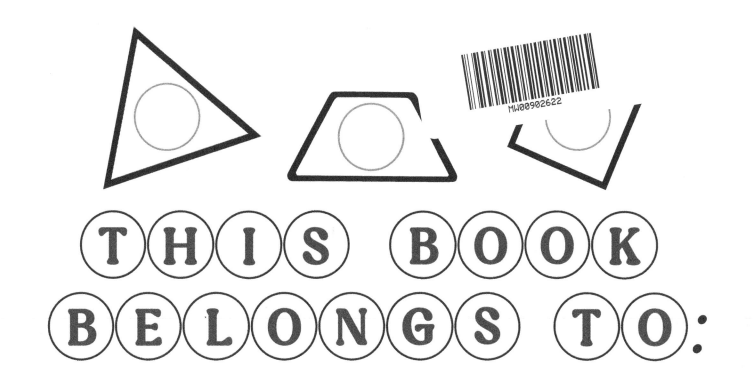

THIS BOOK BELONGS TO:

....

Ⓐ LLIGATOR

DOT ALL THE Ⓐ !

B E A R

DOT ALL THE B !

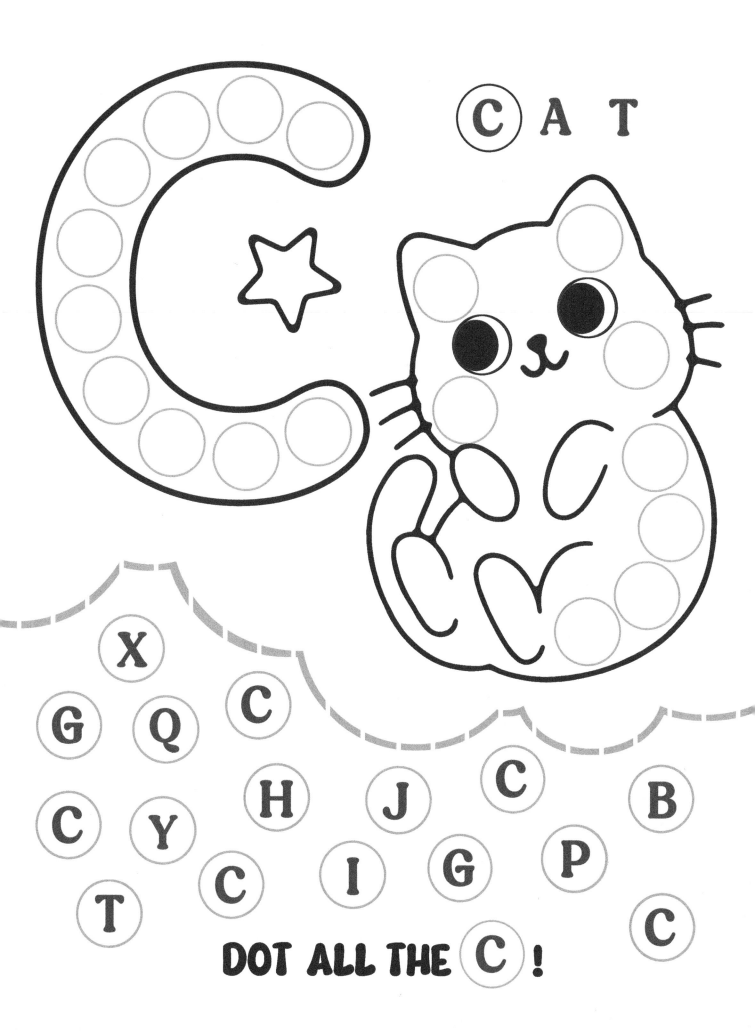

C A T

DOT ALL THE C !

D O G

DOT ALL THE D !

EAGLE

DOT ALL THE E !

F R O G

DOT ALL THE F !

GOOSE

DOT ALL THE G !

HAMSTER

DOT ALL THE (H)!

I GUANA

DOT ALL THE (I)!

JELLYFISH

DOT ALL THE J !

KOALA

DOT ALL THE K !

LION

DOT ALL THE (L)!

MOUSE

DOT ALL THE M !

NARWHAL

DOT ALL THE N !

O W L

DOT ALL THE O !

P

PARROT

K
N
V
P
F
Y
H
P T P
I X O P
P M

DOT ALL THE P !

QUOKKA

DOT ALL THE Q !

RABBIT

DOT ALL THE (R)!

S

(S) S H E E P

E
G
S U
H
D Y S N S L I
S N O T S
S S

DOT ALL THE (S)!

TORTOISE

DOT ALL THE T !

Ⓤ UNICORN

DOT ALL THE Ⓤ !

(V)ULTURE

DOT ALL THE (V)!

W H A L E

DOT ALL THE W !

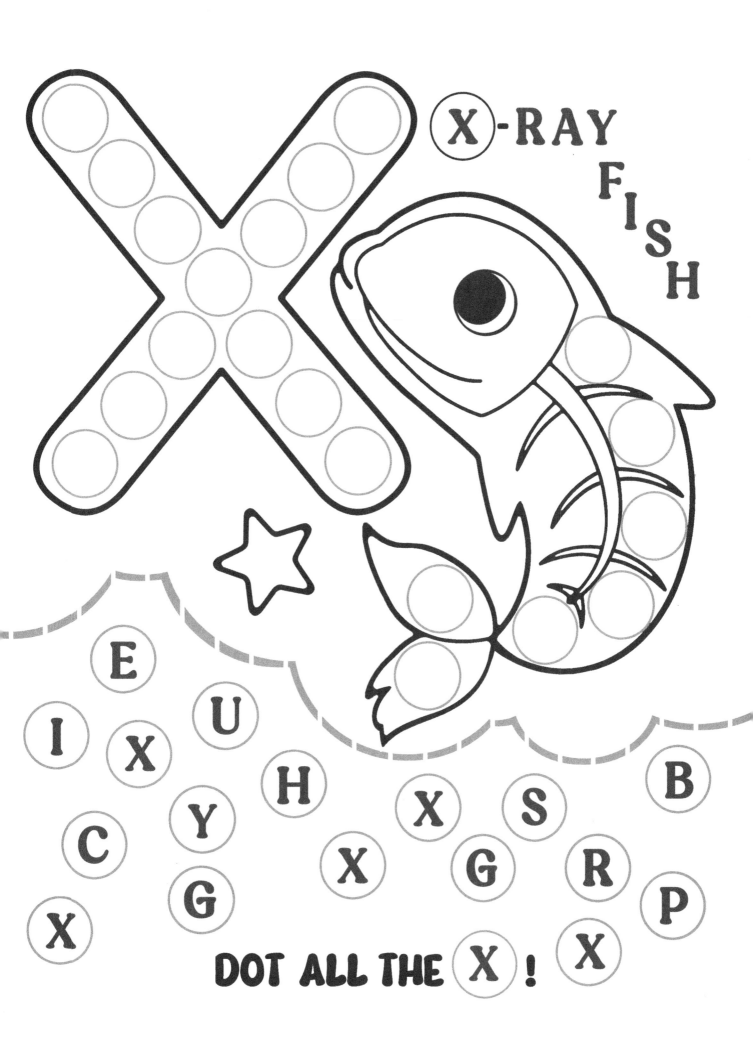

X-RAY FISH

DOT ALL THE (X)!

Y A K

DOT ALL THE Y !

Z ZEBRA

DOT ALL THE Z !

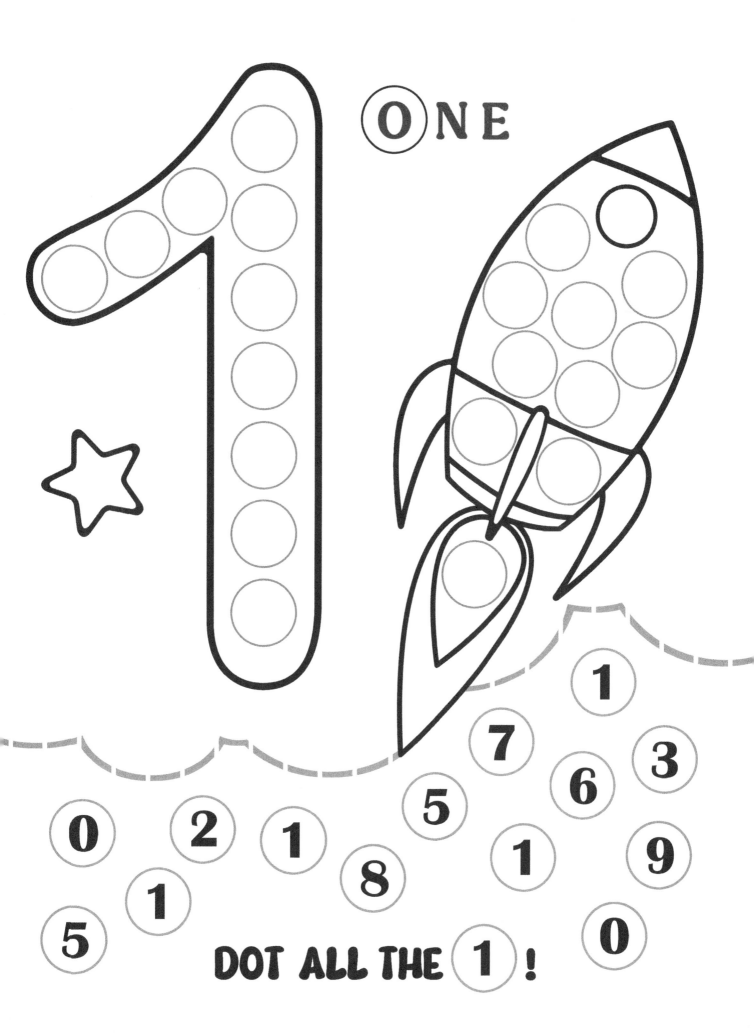

ONE

DOT ALL THE 1 !

TWO

DOT ALL THE 2 !

THREE

DOT ALL THE 3 !

FOUR

DOT ALL THE 4 !

FIVE

DOT ALL THE 5 !

SIX

DOT ALL THE 6 !

SEVEN

DOT ALL THE 7 !

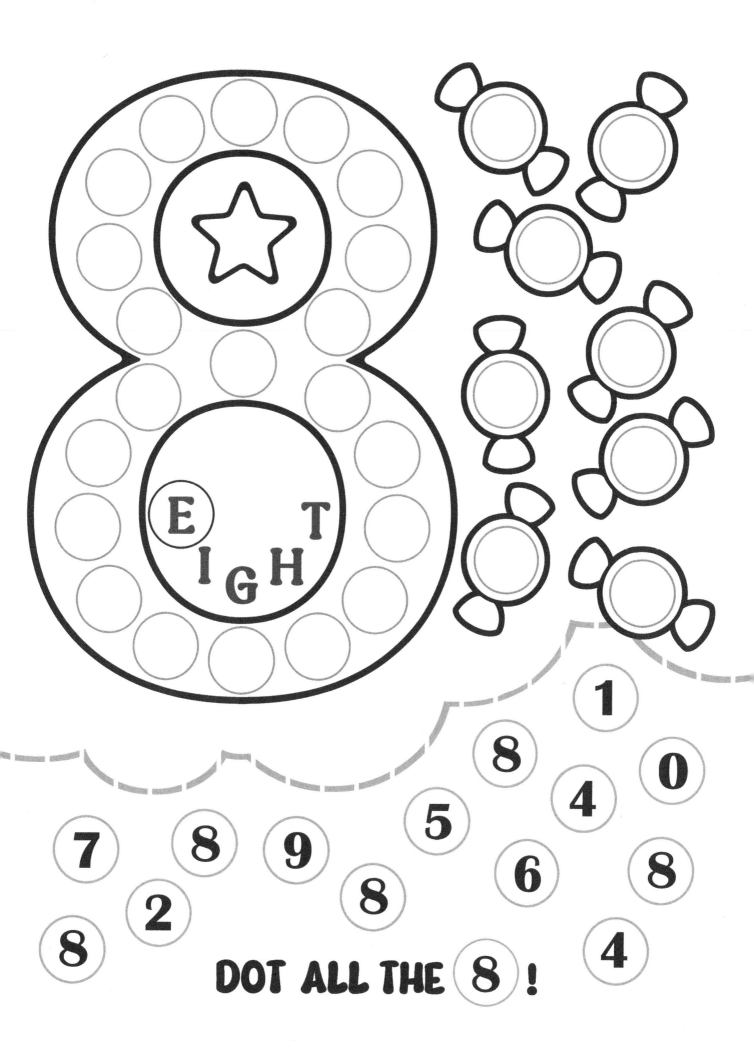

EIGHT

DOT ALL THE 8 !

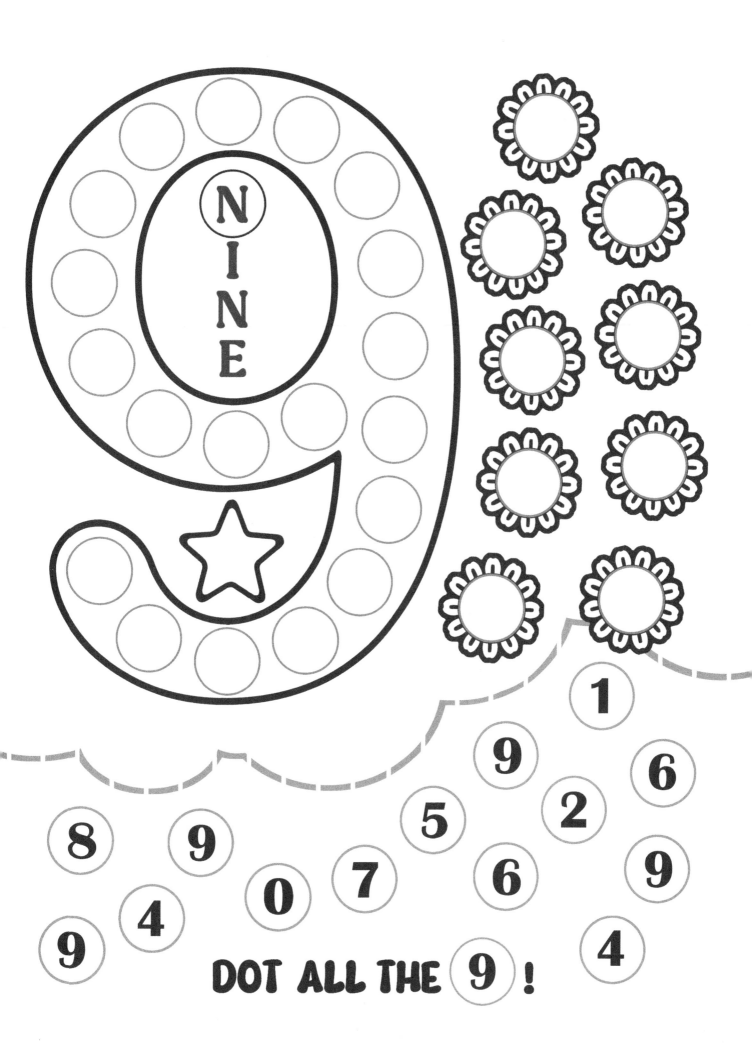

DOT ALL THE 9 !

SHAPES

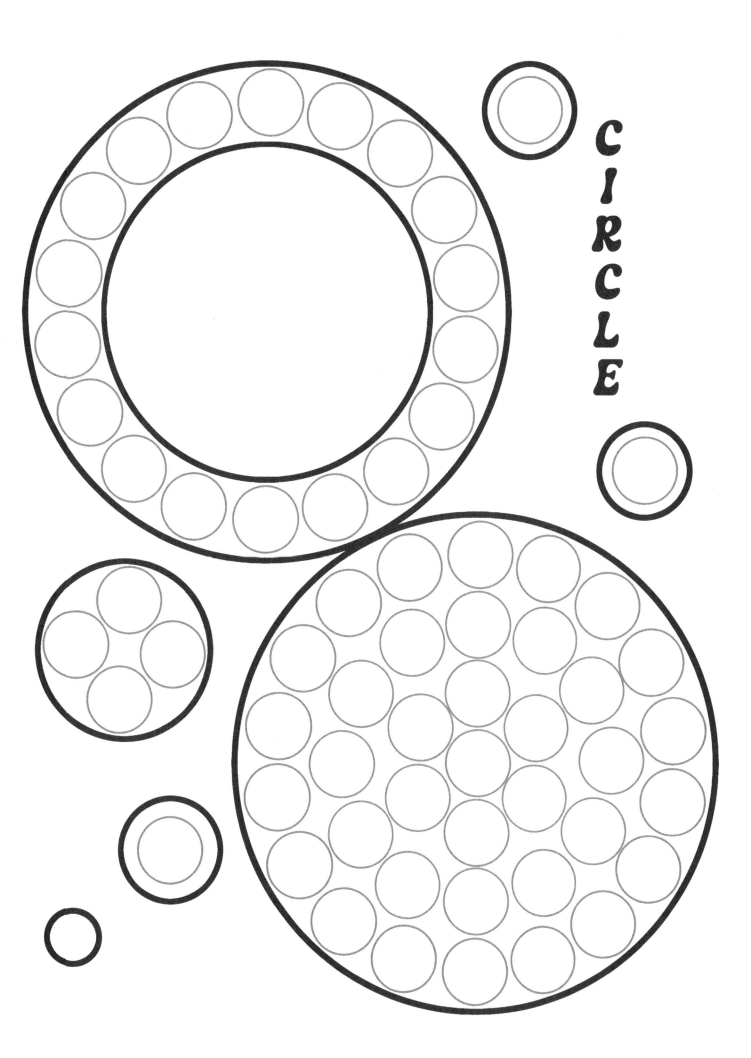

CIRCLE

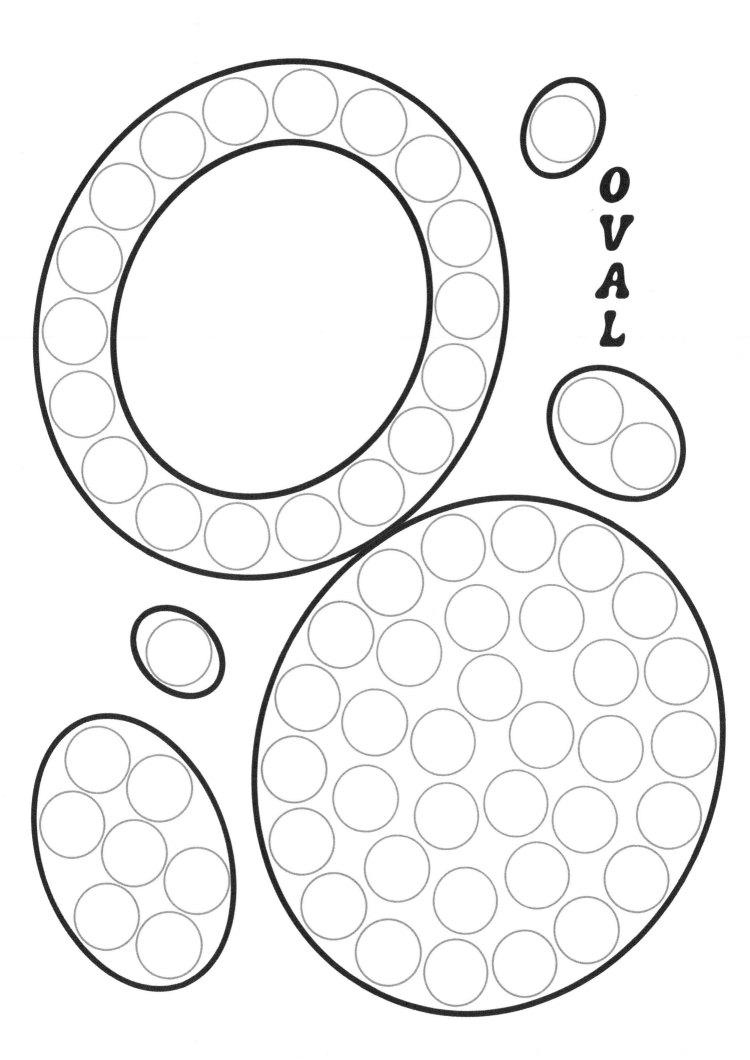

OVAL

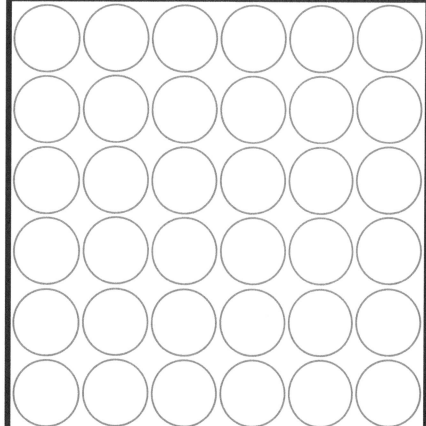

SQUARE

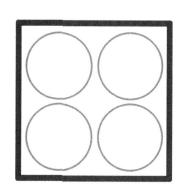

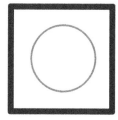

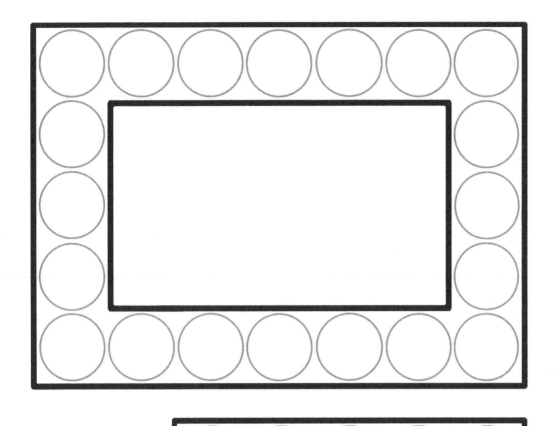

RECTANGLE

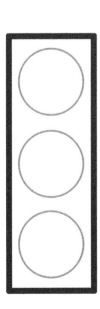

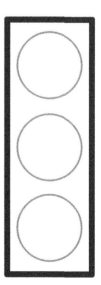

TRIANGLE

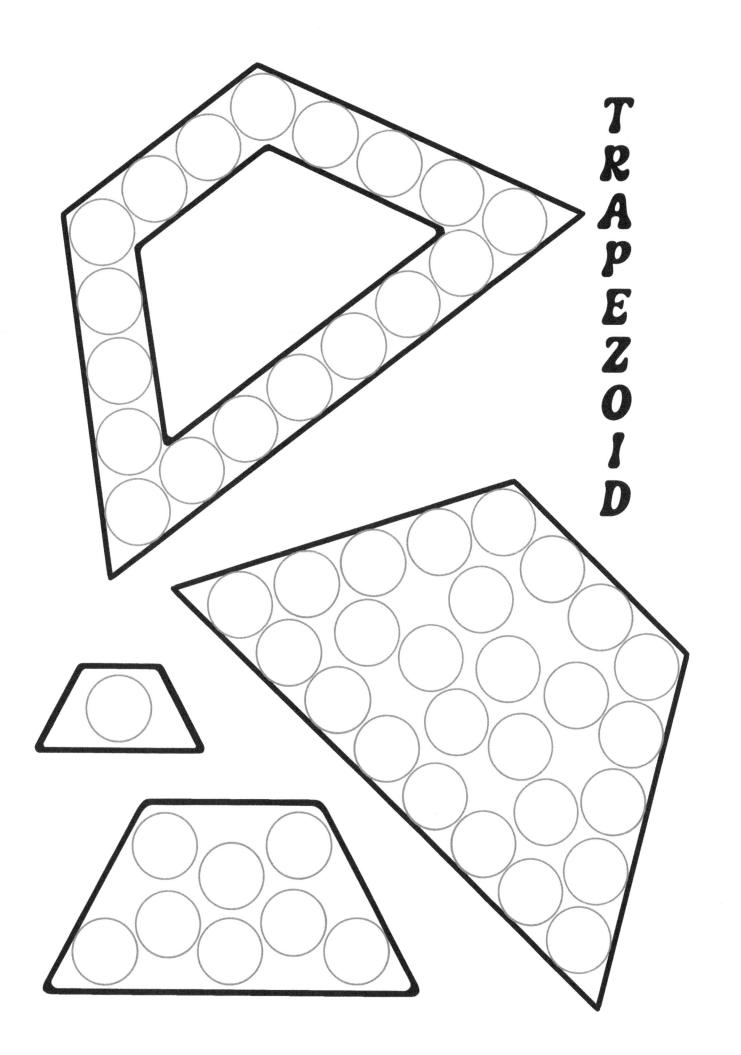

TRAPEZOID

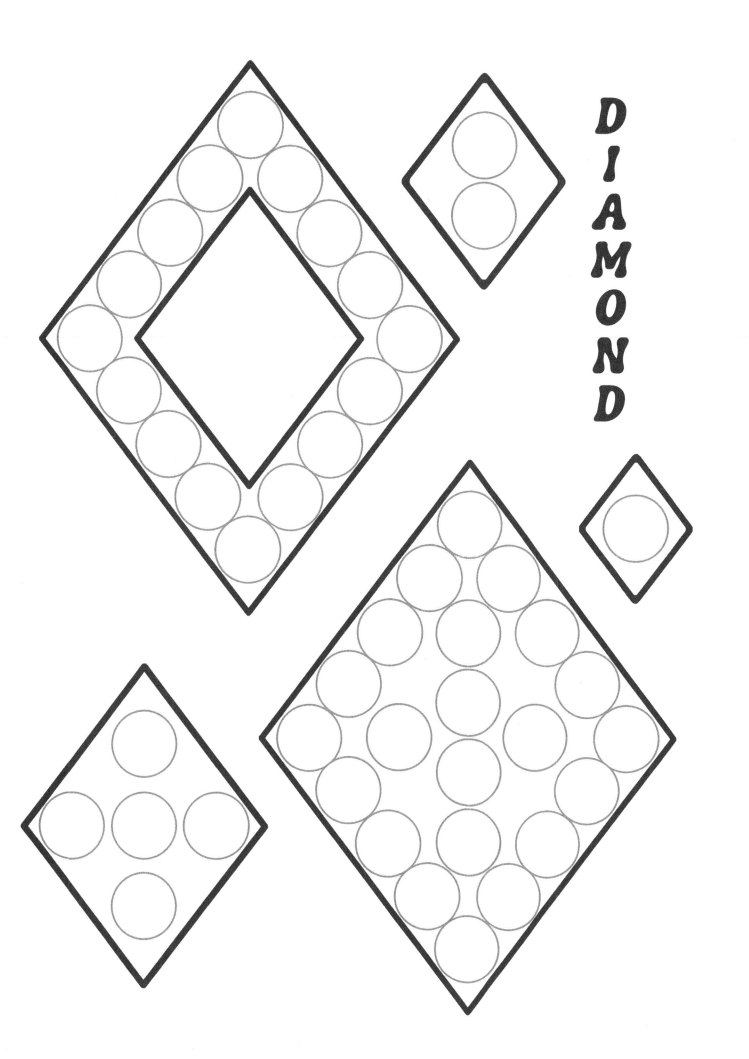

DIAMOND

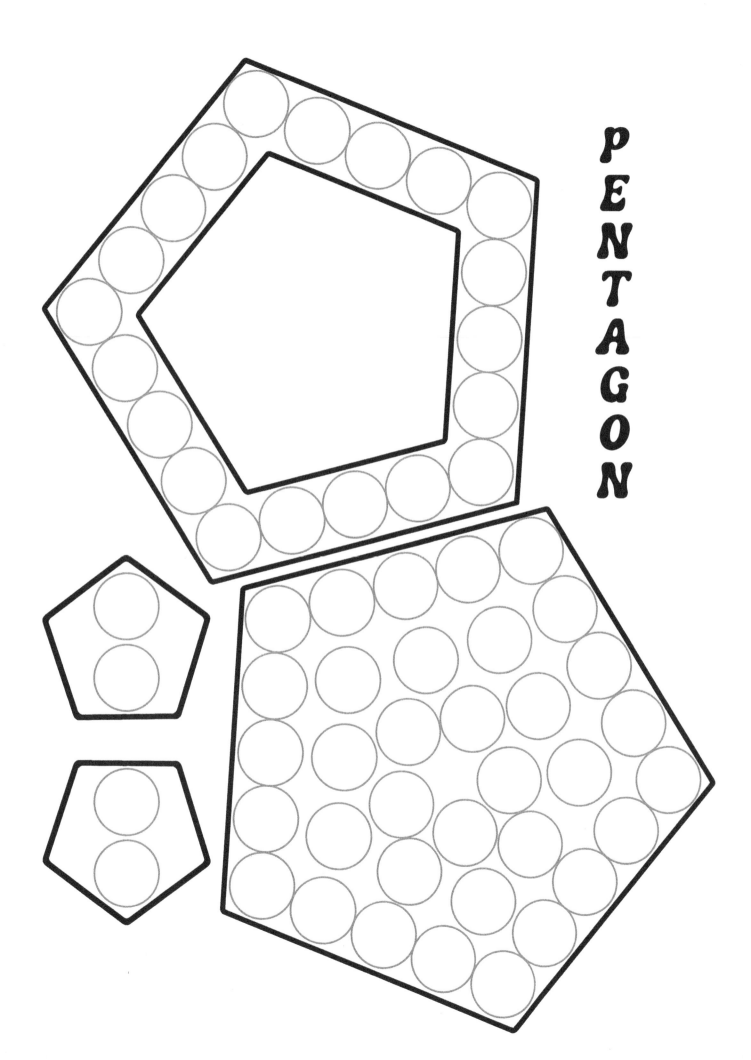

PENTAGON

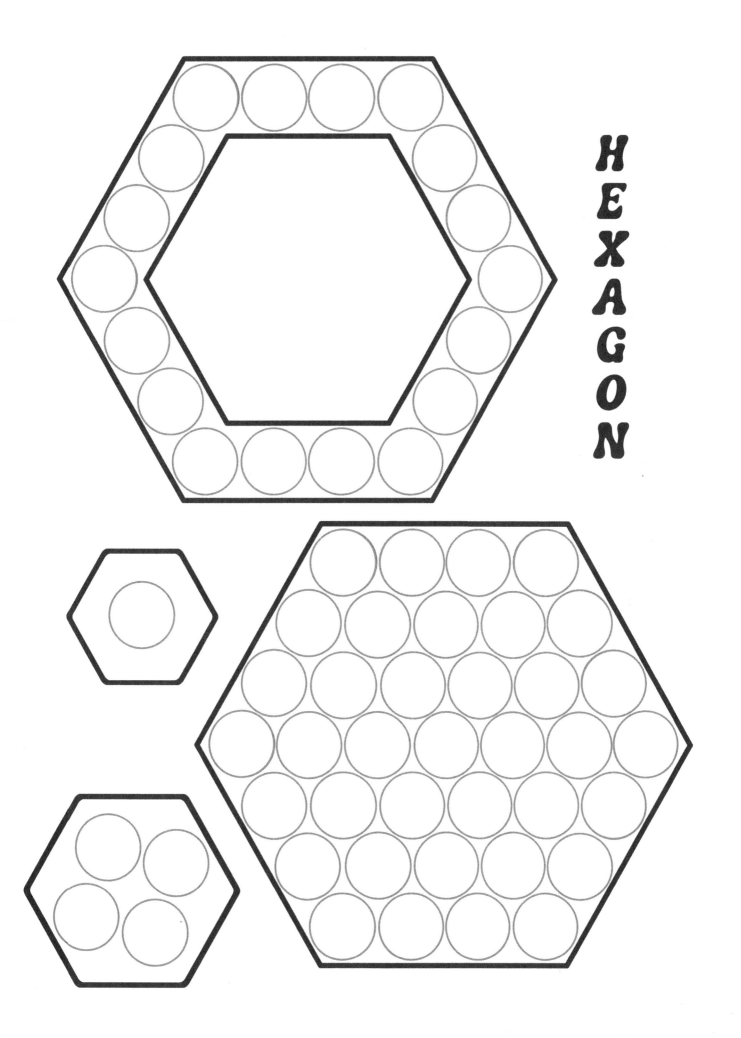

HEXAGON

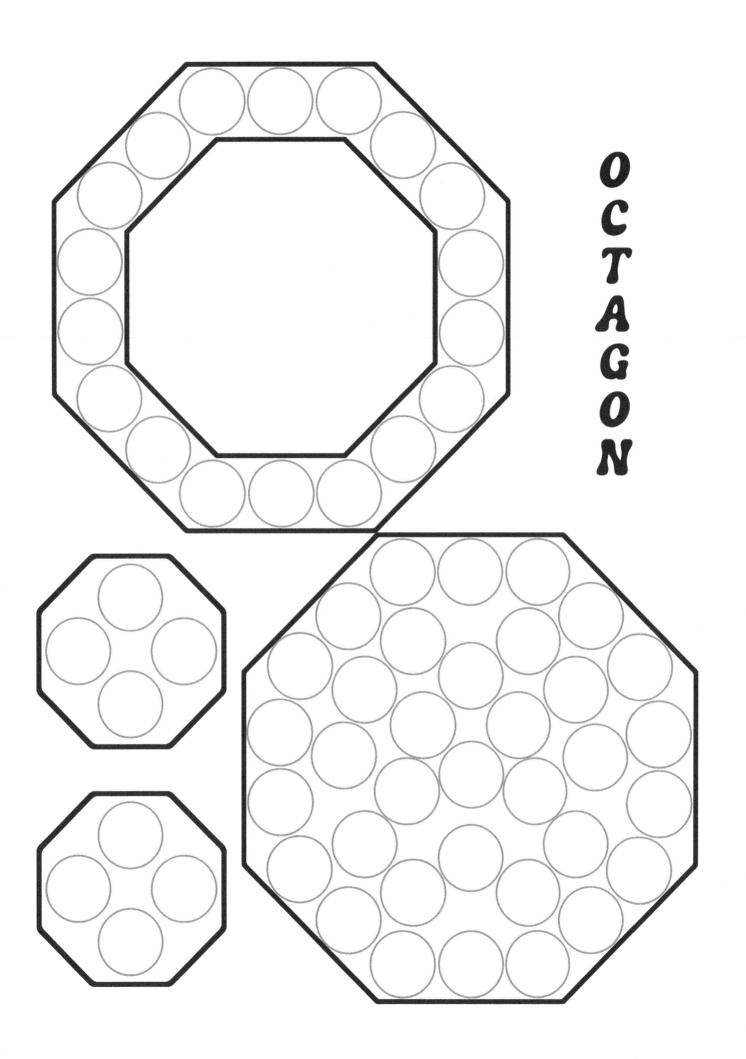

OCTAGON

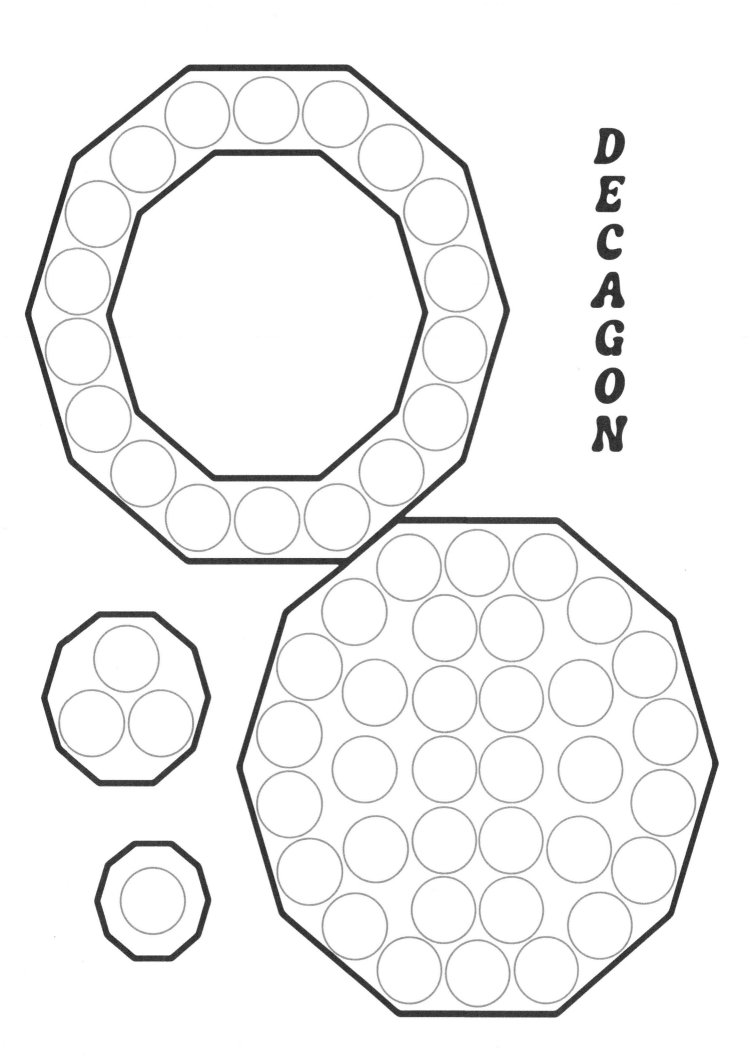

DECAGON

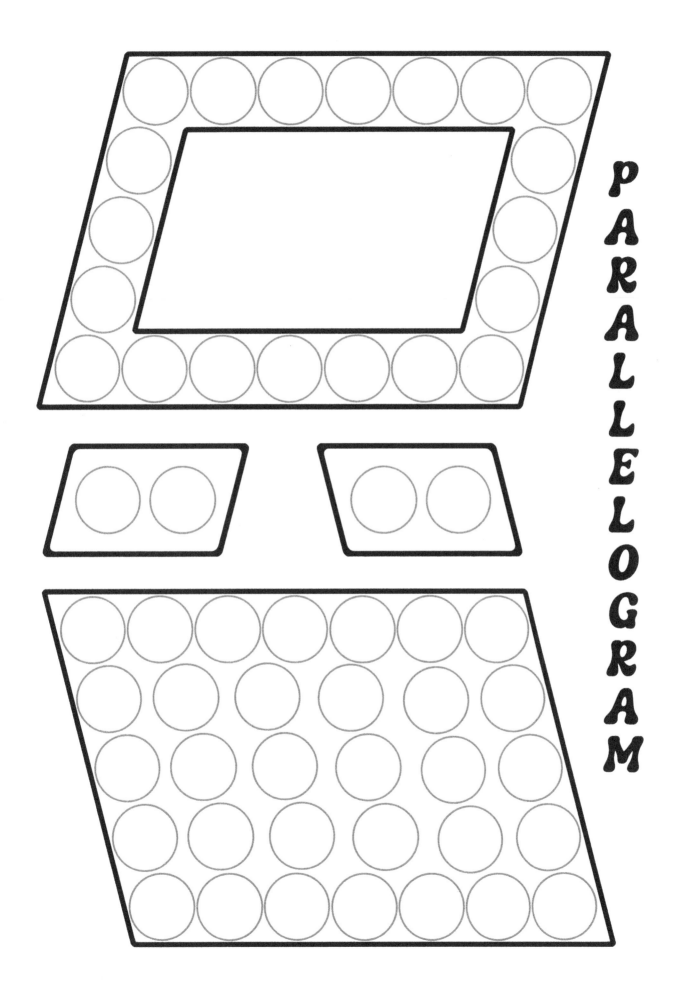

PARALLELOGRAM

STAR

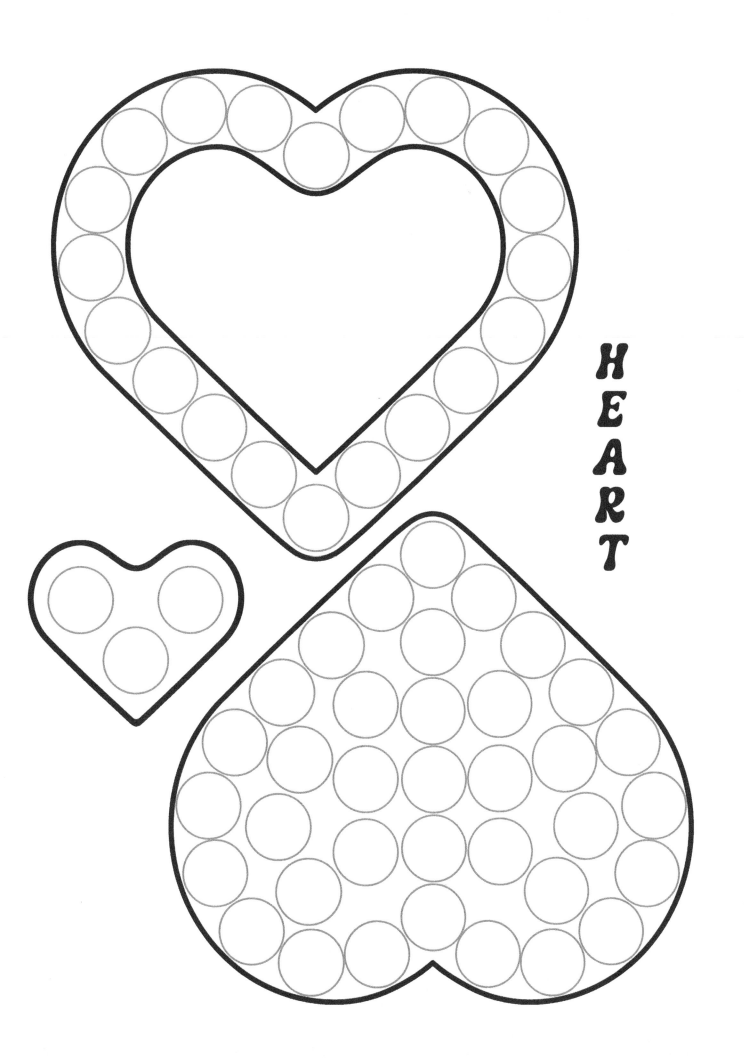

HEART

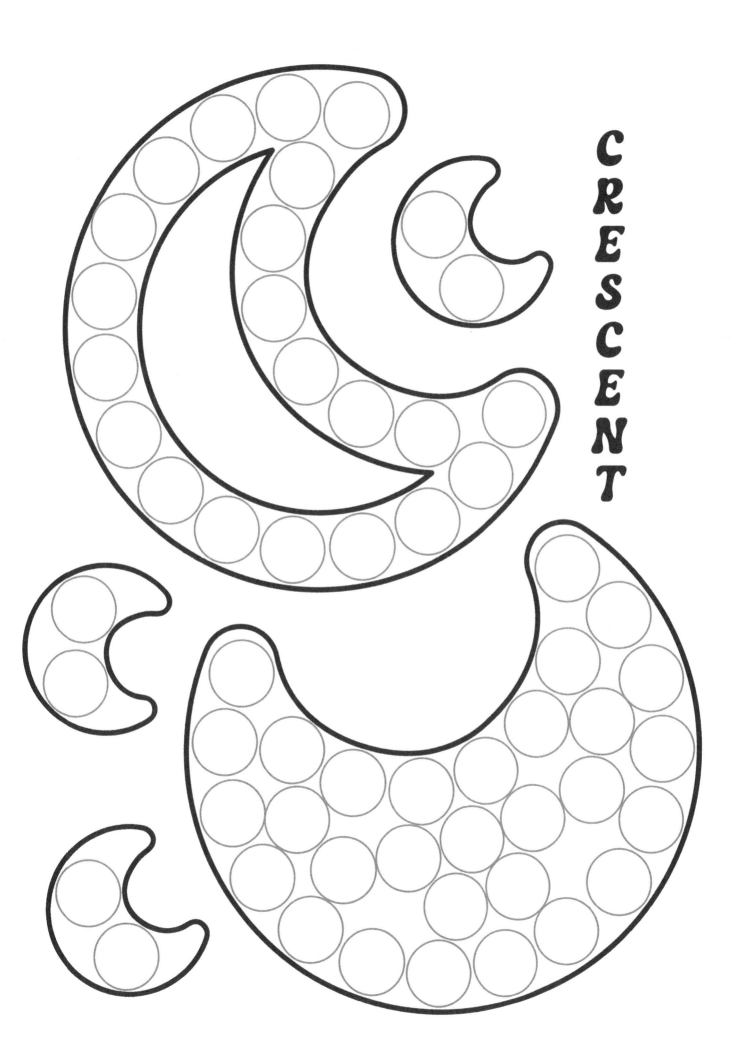

CRESCENT

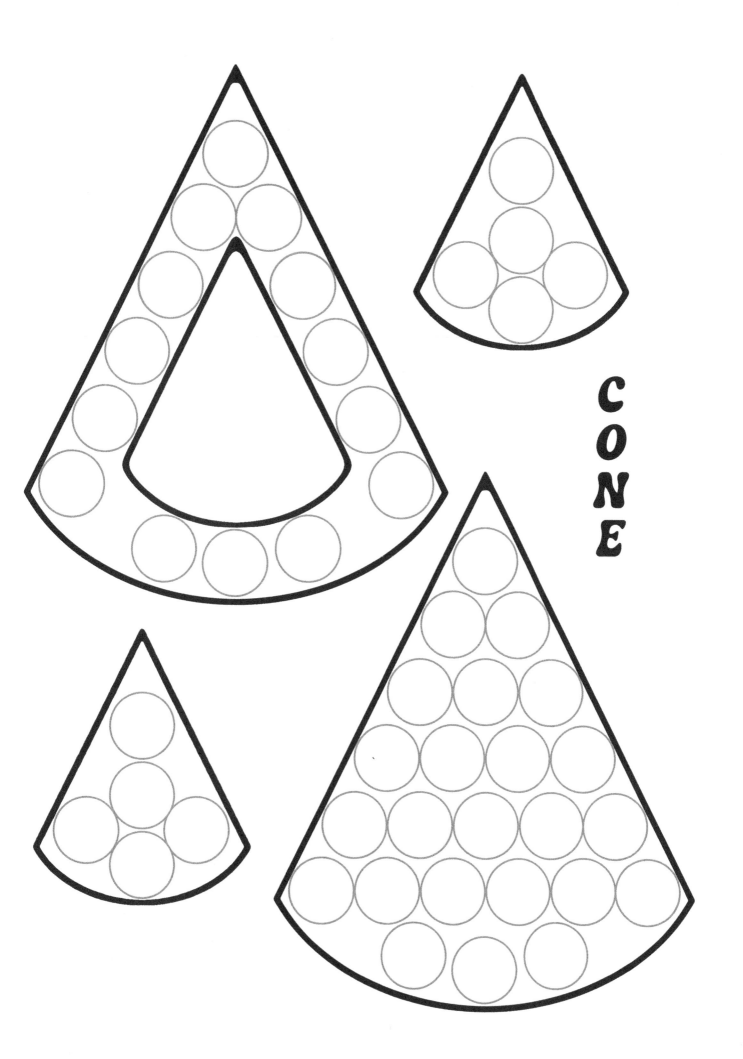

CONE

SEMICIRCLE

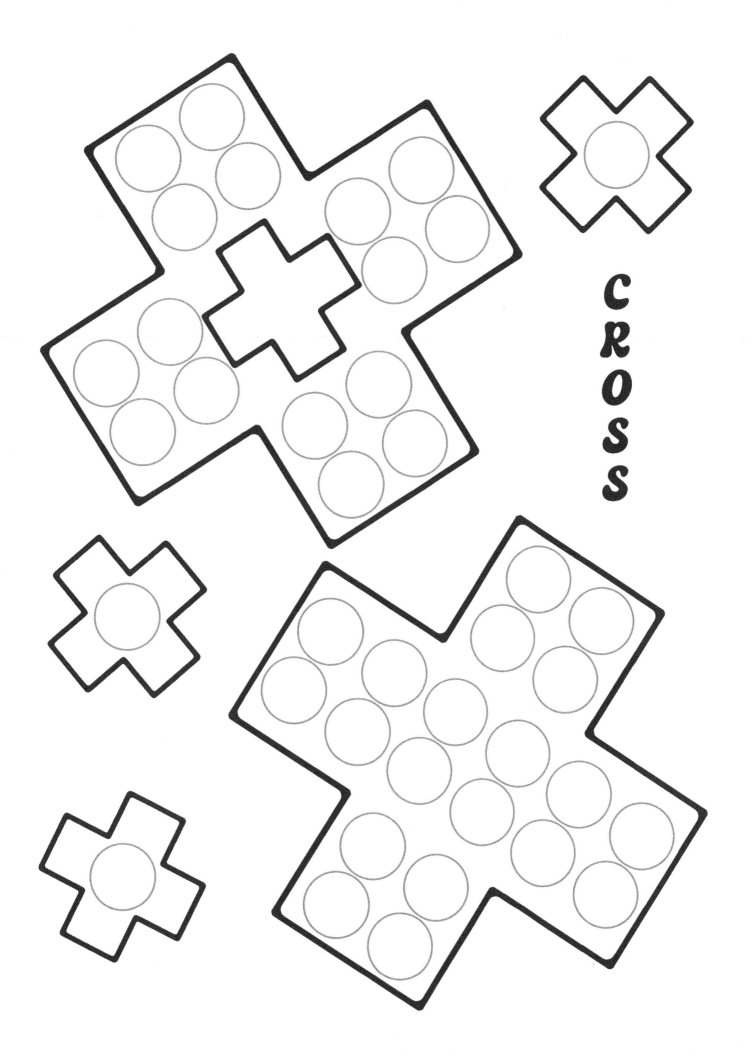

CROSS

CLOUD

BUTTERFLY

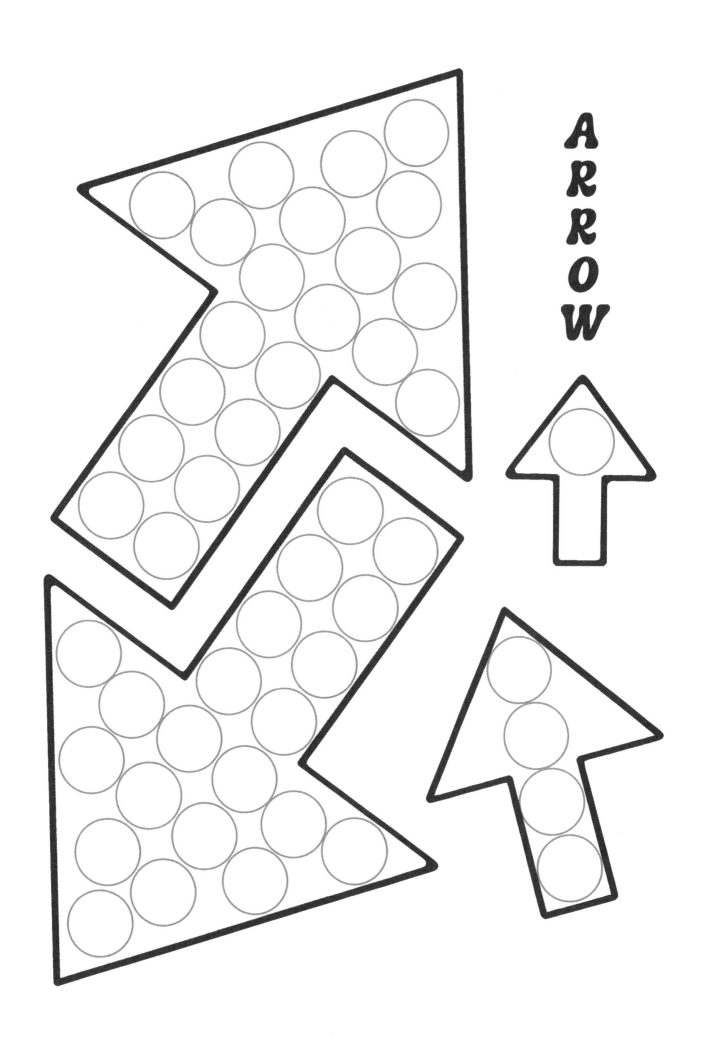

ARROW

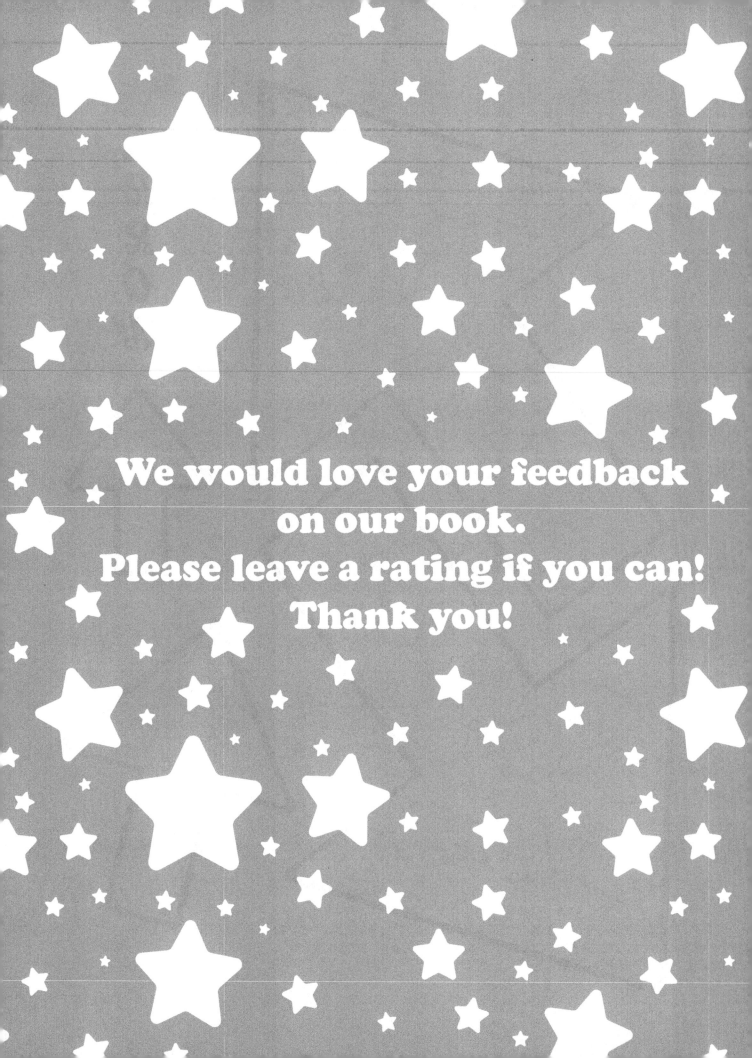

We would love your feedback
on our book.
Please leave a rating if you can!
Thank you!

Made in the USA
Las Vegas, NV
01 December 2024

13138264R00070